GETTING BACK UP!

WHEN LIFE'S PARACHUTES DON'T OPEN.

Myron A. Raney, Ph.D.

EXECUTIVE FOR CHRIST
PUBLISHING GROUP
Columbus, Ohio.

GETTING BACK UP! When Life's Parachutes Don't Open.
by Myron A. Raney, Ph.D.

Published by Executive for Christ Publishing Group
Columbus, Ohio.
Printed in the United States of America.

ISBN: 978-0-9831611-0-3
Library of Congress Control Number: 2013951977

Unless otherwise noted, all scripture is taken from the King James Version of the Bible.

Scripture quotations marked The Amplified Bible or AMP are taken from THE AMPLIFIED BIBLE © 1954, 1958, 1962, 1964, 1965, 1987 by The Lockman Foundation. All rights reserved. Used by permission. (www.Lockman.org).

Cover design by Rockford Penn

Author Contact:

Myron A. Raney, Ph.D.
myron.raney@outlook.com

[Dedication]

This book is dedicated to everyone who has suffered through the experience of having one of life's parachutes fail and has survived the fall, devastating impact, and life changing consequences. Through Christ Jesus you will get back up and you will have the victory!

[Acknowledgements]

My deepest love goes out to our Lord Jesus Christ. I am eternally grateful that you gave me the honor and privilege of receiving your calling, bearing your testimony and sharing Your Word!

I would like to thank my daughter Makayla, my son Mycah, and the rest of my family for being supportive of me over the years and patient with me when I am busy studying and writing. Without you I could not have come this far.

To Debra Ann Jaso, my affection and appreciation for you goes beyond what words can say. I know you will have understanding someday, all in God's time.

Finally, I would like to thank Pastor Rod Parsley and the World Harvest Church Family; also Pastor Rich Nathan and the Vineyard Church of Columbus church family. Your ministries, words of encouragement, and prayers have been pinnacle to my spiritual growth.

[Contents]

[Preface]

This book has a word for both the believer and unbeliever alike. There are many things that Bible scholars disagree about, but there is one thing that they all seem to concur on in agreement, and that is that we are living in the last days. Most of what has been given by inspiration of the Holy Spirit in this message is not what I would call a "new word" from God, but rather a "right now word" from God.

I have watched for years as many of us have been looking for a great outpouring of the Holy Spirit that is promised to usher in a great harvest of souls as we approach the end of time. There is no doubt time is winding up for us, everything around us is just as the Bible foretells things will be in the last days. Matthew 24:3-14 says:

> And as he sat upon the mount of Olives, the disciples came unto him privately, saying, Tell us, when shall these things be? And what shall be the sign of thy coming, and of the end of the world? And Jesus answered and said unto them, Take heed that no man deceive you. For many shall come in my name, say-

ing, I am Christ; and shall deceive many. And ye shall hear of wars and rumors of wars: see that ye be not troubled: for all these things must come to pass, but the end is not yet. For nation shall rise against nation, and kingdom against kingdom: and there shall be famines, and pestilences, and earthquakes, in divers places. All these are the beginning of sorrows. Then shall they deliver you up to be afflicted, and shall kill you: and ye shall be hated of all nations for my name's sake. And then shall many be offended, and shall betray one another, and shall hate one another. And many false prophets shall rise, and shall deceive many. And because iniquity shall abound, the love of many shall wax cold. But he that shall endure unto the end, the same shall be saved. And this gospel of the kingdom shall be preached in all the world for a witness unto all nations; and then shall the end come.

It doesn't take divine discernment to see that time is winding up, but where is this outpouring of the Holy Spirit that the church is waiting for; what's the hold up? After all it is prophesied in the Bible and promises to change church as we have come to know it. Acts 2:17-18 tells us that:

And it shall come to pass in the last days, saith God, I will pour out of my Spirit upon all flesh: and your sons and your daughters shall prophesy, and your young men shall see visions, and your old men shall dream dreams; And on my servants and on my handmaidens I will pour out in those days of my Spirit; and they shall prophesy.

We are crying out for this great outpouring and in so many ways asking God to let it "rain" upon us. We want a fresh anointing; a word from heaven, deeper discernment, showers of blessings, great revivals and the list goes on and on. The Holy Spirit has given me a Word that not only answers why, but provides a solution. This Word from God is a revelation that even though we say we want this great outpouring of the Holy Spirit; the truth is that we are not ready for it and God has shown me why!

In Genesis 2:5 Moses records historical insight to this revelation saying:

And every plant of the field before it was in the earth, and every herb of the field before it grew: for the LORD God had not caused it to rain upon the earth, and there was not a man to till the ground.

God had not caused it to rain upon the earth because there was no man in existence to till the ground. To put it plain and simple, man was not in the position that God needed for him to be in for there to be rain upon the earth. Likewise, we are not in the position today that God needs for us to be in for Him to allow a great downpour. As a whole we are in what I must call a down or fallen position.

The ways we get into that down or fallen state of existences is as numerous as the stars in heaven, but that is not what God wants us to focus on. God wants us to focus on getting back up and into the position that He needs for us to be in. When God does pour out His Spirit He needs for us to be in an upright position ready to help usher in the harvest of souls that the rain will water, nourish, and give new life in Christ Jesus.

This book gives an account of what we will call life's parachutes that the enemy often sabotages causing us to fall; hitting the ground with life changing impact and leaving us hurt, wounded, and out of the position that God needs for us to be in. It is my prayer that through this book you too will find renewed strength to recover from whatever the enemy has sabotaged in your life and get up from your down, lame, or fallen position of inadequacy.

[Prologue]

When God gave me this message he also gave me three mandates. The first was of course to write this book and get it into the hands of as many people within the Body of Christ as possible. The second and most challenging for me was to utilize the concept of "kiss" with this book. That is to say that God wanted me to "keep it short and simple". The third mandate that God gave me concerning this book was for me to not only speak about what He has given me, but to also use what He has given me for myself; we are in this thing together.

As God gave me this message I began to wonder why of all people He would anoint me as the apostle (special messenger) to deliver this message to His people. Just as quickly as I started to ponder over this God gave me the answer and there were two reasons. One, my own life experiences makes it easy to relate to what it means to be in a fallen and down state of existence. Two, although I thought I was in a position to be totally used of God; the truth was that I was still not in the position God needed for me to be in for Him to use me to the fullest.

The truth of the matter is that even though I thought I was sold out for Christ I really wasn't because I was still in a lame position rather that the position God needed for me to be in. That's right, because of some things that the enemy had sabotaged in my life I was in what God called a lame (fallen, down, broken, inadequate) position. I was still bound by past hurts, brokenness, and fear. For the most part I was fine but there were still some wounds that prohibited me from standing up and fully getting into the position that God needed me to be in.

The Holy Spirit brought to my remembrance the story about a certain man over in the book of Acts. We can find his story in Acts 3:2-7 which says:

> And a certain man lame from his mother's womb was carried, whom they laid daily at the gate of the temple which is called Beautiful, to ask alms of them that entered into the temple; who seeing Peter and John about to go into the temple asked an alms. And Peter, fastening his eyes upon him with John, said, Look on us. And he gave heed unto them, expecting to receive something of them. Then Peter said, Silver and

gold have I none; but such as I have give I thee: In the name of Jesus Christ of Nazareth rise up and walk. And he took him by the right hand, and lifted him up: and immediately his feet and ankle bones received strength.

There was nothing wrong with this man according to the Bible with the exception that he had weak feet and ankle bones that prohibited him from getting up and being a productive member of society. The enemy sabotaged a particular area of his life from birth and for many years he would lay at the gates daily in a lame position begging to receive something; anything that he could get.

But then on that faithful afternoon this man who was lame at the gate encountered Peter and John who gave him more than he anticipated that day. They gave him a touch from God in the name of Jesus Christ of Nazareth that set him in an upright position to go leaping and praising God. On that day his life was changed forever. On that day, in the name of Jesus, he got up!

The main difference between the man at the gate and us is that he was born into this world in a lame position and we at some point fall into a lame position. Our lame position is the result of a fall that we take in life and fail to get back up from. We too can get back up and into the position that God wants us to be in. Just as the man at the gates got up in the name of Jesus we too should be getting up in the name of Jesus.

As quickly as God gave me this revelation He also gave me the concept of Parachutes. At first I marveled at the idea but could not see the significance until by His divine plan I came across the story of a young woman who because of her testimony I will call Tessa, who jumped out of an airplane and fell ten thousand feet without a functioning parachute. She lived and remarkably got back up in spite of her massive injuries. What God has shown me that I must now share with you is that the hardest thing about falling is getting back up. Just know that In the name of Jesus we can; to be in the position God needs us to be in we must!

[Introduction]

The hardest part about falling in any given situation is getting back up. That is because when we fall, we often get hurt in the process and end up either wounded or injured. There is no doubt that falling is often a traumatic experience for most of us. However, one thing that is for certain is that a fall is a prerequisite for an opportunity to get back up. We can never have an opportunity to get back up if we don't fall first.

Many times in life we find ourselves in the midst of a great fall. The kind of fall that I am talking about is not a physical fall, but rather a fall from a certain place that we desire to be, or rather where we think we should be. At worst case scenario we fall from a place that we need to be or from where God needs for us to be.

By natural design we are made to get back up when we fall. The problem is that all too often we fall, but don't get back up. If we don't get back up we are not in the position that God needs for us to be. When we fall, in our minds we believe that we have gotten back up, but in reality we just learn to adapt to our new found down position.

This is where the problem is. You see, I can pretty much guarantee that any time we take a fall in life Satan, also known as the enemy, is behind it in one way or another. Not only that, once we have fallen the enemy gets very busy in doing everything that he can to make sure that we stay down. Satan does everything from adding insult to injury to suggesting to us that we can't get back up. The enemy would have us to believe that we have fallen for the last time to rise no more.

It is easy for us to believe this lie from the pits of hell because of how we feel after a fall. Often times we feel broken in our spirit, depressed, wounded emotionally, and even physical sickness can manifest itself in our natural bodies. Over the years I have encountered many people who have fallen and have yet to get back up. To make matters worse, they have not even begun the process of getting back up. I myself have even been one of those people.

One evening when I was praying, the Lord began to speak to me about the multitudes of people in the Body of Christ who are broken, wounded, and still grounded as a result of past failures in life, referred to from now on as falls.

The Holy Spirit imparted in me a word that is not necessarily a new word, but a right now word. I learned a long time ago that what we often need is not necessarily a new word from God, but rather a right now word from God. That is a word that has meaning and immediate application to our life.

The Holy Spirit began to show me that for us to know all the possible falls that we can encounter in life is not important. It isn't even important to visit all the falls of our past because it is just that, the past. But one thing that God wants us to know is that it's what we put our trust in other than Him that enables the enemy to cause us to fall. With this the Holy Spirit enlightened me with the concept of parachutes and the process of getting back up.

The Holy Spirit led me to see the significance of parachutes not just in the natural, but also in a spiritual sense. If you jump out of an airplane in the natural and your parachute fails to open, you are going to fall to the ground with a devastating life changing, if not deadly consequences. Likewise, if the parachutes we choose in life fail to open, we fall and are left to endure painful and often life changing consequences.

The things in life that we put our trust in other than God is what I have been led to call parachutes. When the enemy sabotages our parachutes and they fail to open, quite simply we find ourselves hurting. I won't give the enemy all the credit because Satan can't do anything to us that we don't let him do. Understand that we set ourselves up to have our parachutes sabotaged simply by the parachutes we choose; the things other than God we put our trust in.

For those of us who have a need to be academically correct in regards to what a parachute is and how this concept is relative to this book I have included this little lesson. The word parachute is a hybrid of words coined by a French aeronaut named Francois Blanchard in 1785. The etymology of the word parachute reveals that it generally means "that which protects against a fall."

The first half of the word "para" comes from the Latin word parare which means to defend against. The remainder of the word "chute" means a fall. In more literal terms a parachute is designed to help you defend against a fall. The reason why God gave me the "parachute concept" should by now be dropping in your spirit as well.

In this book when we talk about one of "life's parachutes" we are referring to those things in life that we put our trust in hoping that they will defend us against a fall or failure of one type or another. In many ways they can be compared to the parachutes that skydivers trust when jumping out of an airplane to deliver them safely to the ground. It doesn't matter if it was at a local air show or on television, I believe we have all seen a parachute in action and can relate to the contrast between life's parachutes and literal parachutes.

Like so many things in life, parachutes are colorful, exciting, and spectacular to watch. To skydivers, parachutes are absolutely essential to survival. Parachutes come in a variety of shapes, colors, and technical configurations depending on their purpose and intended functionality. Skydivers are trained to trust parachutes with their very lives. They depend on parachutes to catch them from a death defying free fall and deliver them safely to the hard ground several thousand feet below.

Although they are not literal parachutes, all of us have parachutes in our lives that we depend on. They are the things in our lives that we trust will catch us, break our fall, and carry us to a place of happily ever after when we take a leap of faith into life's great unknown adventures and ambitions. Like real parachutes, the parachutes in our lives come in a variety of shapes, sizes, and configurations; depending upon the purpose they have and the fall that they are suppose to protect us from. They come in the forms of our education, careers, friendships, marriages, businesses, and yes even religious affiliations to name a few. We trust that at some point they will fully deploy, break our free falls in life, and deliver us safely to the ground. In other words, delivering us to that place of happily ever after where we desire to be.

But all too often our parachutes fail to deploy and we find ourselves free falling out of control towards the cold hard ground below. The things that we trust most; our education, careers, friendships, marriages, businesses, and even our religious affiliations fail to fully open up. Our parachutes fail to carry us to that place of happily ever after where we expect to land. As a result, we inevitably hit the ground of reality with blunt force and life changing impact.

Upon impact, we find ourselves broken, wounded, and full of devastation. We find ourselves in immense pain. We are critically injured emotionally, spiritually, psychologically, and sometimes even physically. The blunt force of the impact leaves us lifeless in so many ways and in a lame position.

With the life knocked out of us, we have little to no desire to be moved, let alone get up. We find ourselves in critical condition, on spiritual life support, laid out in the intensive care unit of disappointment. As we begin to recover we often have little to no desire to leap out on faith towards the adventurous things in life ever again. We simply don't have much faith in those all alluring life parachutes anymore that we once trusted. Simply stated, we are not thinking about getting back up.

The post traumatic effect is almost unbearable because many of us have been taught that as children of God life will be so much better than where we are now. That everything will always be just fine because we are the righteousness of God. We forget that the word of God warns us that, "Many are the afflictions of the righteous . . ." (Psalm 34:19).

It is at this point that Satan gets real busy in hindering our recovery. Keep in mind that there is a 100% chance that Satan has already played a part in our fall to begin with one way or another. The Gospel according to John tells us that, "The thief cometh not, but for to steal, and to kill, and to destroy. . ." (John 10:10). In the shadows of our traumatic experiences Satan would have us to remain in a broken, wounded, and in a depressed and devastated state of existence. Satan's intention is to magnify our pain, increase our suffering, and steal from us any desire to rise above life's tragedies and walk in the fullness and abundance of God's purpose for our lives.

When our parachutes don't open, it is God's desire for us to survive the impact, arise from the devastation, heal, and prepare for our next leap of faith into life's great adventures. It is God's will that we be made whole again, get back up, and experience all that life has to offer. In the same passage of scripture, the Gospel according to John gives us assurance of this saying, ". . . I came that they might have life, and that they might have it more abundantly." (John 10:10).

This book is not designed to be an in-depth examination about what causes parachutes in our life not to open. We have already established that it is a safe bet that whatever has caused the malfunction; Satan has played a role in it somewhere along the line so we can just leave it at that. Also, this book does not set out to identify all the potential parachute failures that we may possibly encounter in life or how to avoid them. So what in the world is this book about?

This is a prolific book inspired by the Holy Spirit about survival, perseverance, and triumph. Using the real life events of one woman's tragic fall during a skydiving accident, God gives us the revelation that life is full of parachutes that we depend on every day that from time to time fail to open leaving us to fall with life changing consequences.

Satan in all his insidiousness is forever busy trying to sabotage out parachutes, plotting a fall in our life in hopes that your fall will leave you so broken and wounded that you will rise no more and never get in the position that God needs for you to be. If we are not careful Satan will find ways to sabotage our parachutes. The enemy will sabotage our educational endeavors, careers, friendships, marriages, businesses, and even our religious affiliations.

But we can give thanks to God that when we fall we are afforded many opportunities to get back up. Despite what the enemy does in our life or whispers in our ear the Bible tells us, "For a just man falleth seven times, and riseth up again. . ." (Proverbs 24:16). In this book God gives us a message that empowers us to fall, get back up, and in the words of the prophet Micah proclaim, "Rejoice not against me, O mine enemy: When I fall, I shall arise. . ." (Micah 7:8).

Part I
When Parachutes Fail

[Chapter 1]

Getting Understanding

"The beginning of Wisdom is: get Wisdom (skillful and godly Wisdom)! [For skillful and godly Wisdom is the principal thing.] And with all you have gotten, get understanding (discernment, comprehension, and interpretation)."
(Proverbs 4:7, AMP).

It is important for you to understand exactly what I am talking about in this book when I speak interchangeably about "parachutes" and "life parachutes". The simplistic definition of a parachute does not provide the kind of understanding needed to properly set the stage for the remainder of discussions in this book.

Again, Proverbs 4:7 in the Amplified Bible says, "The beginning of Wisdom is: get Wisdom (skillful and godly Wisdom)! [For skillful and godly Wisdom is the principal thing.] And with all you have gotten, get understanding (discernment, comprehension, and interpretation)." Having reemphasized what is needed let's move forward to get that understanding.

The primary definition of a parachute according to the Merriam-Webster dictionary is that it is a piece of equipment usually made of cloth that is fastened to people or things and that allows them to fall slowly and land safely after they have jumped or been dropped from an aircraft. This definition may seem adequate enough in almost any explanation but I find it necessary to provide the etymology of the word parachute. It may seem somewhat elementary to visit definitions in such detail but you will appreciate the purpose, meaning, and relevance as time goes on.

The word parachute is a hybrid of words coined by a French aeronaut named Francois Blanchard in 1785. The etymology of the word parachute reveals that it generally means "that which protects against a fall." The first half of the word "para" comes from the Latin word parare which means to defend against. The remainder of the word "chute" means a fall. In more literal terms a parachute is designed to help you defend against a fall.

In life there are many things that we pack as parachutes before jumping out into the big blue sky of life. These are what I commonly refer to as our "life parachutes". Our parachutes come in the form of our education, careers, relationships, and affiliations just to name a few. They give us a false sense of security believing that since we have them packed away in our backpacks that they will protect and defend us against a fall.

As we will soon discover, when a parachute or life parachute does not open or defend us against a fall, the results are devastating to say the least. It is worth noting here that the resulting fall from a failed parachute can be a spiritual, emotional, social, economical, or even a physical fall.

[Chapter 2]

Tessa's Testimony

"And they have overcome (conquered) him by means of the blood of the Lamb and by the utterance of their testimony, for they did not love and cling to life even when faced with death [holding their lives cheap till they had to die for their witnessing]." (Revelation 12:11, AMP).

O nce in a while you find a story that is so remarkable that it leaves you in a state of near disbelief. Often times we will find such a story and neglect to realize that it is actually a testimony. Of course everyone's story can be a testimony of one magnitude or another.

When God gave me the concept of the parachute, the Holy Spirit led me to this story. This story, which as you soon will discover is one of the most remarkable testimonies that could have ever been told. This testimony sets the tone for the remainder of the book and holds more significance than one could ever imagine. For in this testimony we can truly see God at work, and get an understanding of how we can survive life's falls and get back up.

The Word of God tells us in the book of Revelation that we can overcome not only by the blood of the Lamb, but also by the utterance of our testimonies (Revelation 12:11). In other words, when we hear of another person's testimony, it gives us the strength to overcome and to conquer the enemy. This is the story of one woman's experience that provides us with a testimony by which we can gain strength and encouragement to overcome the pain, devastation, and consequences of a fall.

On October 9, 2005 a young woman from Joplin, Missouri who we will call Tessa prepared herself to make her first 10,000 foot accelerated free fall skydive. This was her first time making the jump solo. Just to clarify, it was her first time making the jump unassisted and alone. Full of excitement, Tessa was confident that she was well prepared for the jump she was about to make. Why wouldn't she be? Tessa had spent countless hours learning everything she needed to know about skydiving and had completed nine successful assisted jumps prior to this day.

Having traveled to Siloam Springs, Arkansas, Tessa boarded the airplane as she had previously done many times before. Within moments, the small plane was speeding down the runway and ultimately lifted off the ground making its ascent into the clear blue sky. By this time there is no doubt that Tessa had already made all of her safety checks and was beginning to mentally prepare herself for the impending first solo accelerated free fall skydive that she had long anticipated.

As the plane traveled upward to 2,000 feet, then to 4,000 feet, and then to 6,000 feet, Tessa was probably beginning to imagine exactly what the jump was going to be like. She could see herself standing in the porthole of the airplane, leaping out into the clear blue sky, falling with the crisp refreshing wind blowing against her face, and at the appointed time deploying her parachute that would gently carry her safely to the ground below. The airplane continued its climb past 8,000 feet and then arrived at its destination of 10,000 feet. Finally, it was time to jump!

Full of confidence and having full faith in her parachute, Tessa proceeded to the porthole, took a deep breath, exhaled, and jumped out of the plane into the deep blue yonder. Just as she had imagined, she found herself free falling with the crisp cool wind rushing against her face. She could see the ground below racing towards her. For approximately 35 seconds she fell with nothing between her and the ground but air. As she approached 6,000 feet Tessa prepared to deploy her parachute which she had learned over time to fully trust with her life.

As with her nine previous jumps, Tessa had full faith in her parachute. She trusted that when she deployed her chute that it was going to open up, break her fall, and carry her safely down to earth. In full confidence and believing she was in full control, Tessa pulled her rip cord to deploy her parachute. As she anticipated, her parachute opened, and from all indications this jump was going to be just like her last nine jumps.

Feeling a false sense of security, Tessa prepared herself to settle down and enjoy the scenery as she began to slow down and drift towards the inviting ground below. Could this first solo free fall truly go so smoothly for the young skydiver? Was this jump truly going to go as smoothly as Tessa's nine previous jumps? In just a matter of a few brief seconds, Tessa would experience an unprecedented turn of events that would change her life forever.

Suddenly, Tessa was faced with the hard reality that her decent back to earth was not going to be smooth sailing. In an instant, she had to come to the realization that something was going terribly wrong. She heard a snap and started spinning rapidly out of control; gaining acceleration as she began to plummet towards the ground.

When Tessa looked up at her parachute, she discovered that her steering toggle had snapped and her canopy was in danger of totally collapsing which would create an even more life threatening situation. Tessa's trusty parachute, in which she had full faith, had failed putting her very life in danger.

Having been trained for such an emergency, Tessa immediately took action to save her life and cut away her main parachute in preparation to deploy her reserve parachute. Still feeling somewhat confident that she could return back down to earth safely, Tessa then deployed her reserve parachute. As fate would have it, the reserve parachute too failed to properly deploy. Tessa was still falling rapidly out of control towards the ground below. Tessa now very quickly came to the realization that the parachutes that she had once trusted and had full faith in had both failed her.

Tessa was almost in a state of sheer disbelief. First, her main parachute had failed and then her backup chute had failed as well. What were the odds of that happening? Experts agree that the chances of a parachute failing are about one in a million. However, the odds of both parachutes failing are almost nonexistent.

Now falling from initially about 10,000 feet without a functional parachute, Tessa makes one last attempt to break her fall by pumping the brakes on her backup parachute in an effort to get it to fully deploy. When her backup parachute still failed to fully deploy, Tessa began to accept the reality of the grim situation she was in.

Tessa realized that she was in a free fall from 10,000 feet. She realized that she was diving solo, so for all intended purposes she was in fact alone, falling from heights not generally survived. To that end she began to accept the fact that she was most likely going to die in a few short moments.

Having done all that she could at that point to save herself, Tessa totally let go of her parachute's steering toggles thinking to herself, "I'm going to die. I'm going to hit the ground. I'm going to die." While still falling, Tessa made her petition known to God. She asked God, "Please take away the pain of the impact." She told God, "I am ready to go home, but I just don't want to feel the pain." Having now made her peace with God, accepting that she was going to impact the ground all alone and die, Tessa then laid herself out into a prostrate position, belly-to-earth, closed her eyes, and fell to the earth from 10,000 feet without a functioning parachute.

Tessa landed in a blacktopped parking lot impacting the ground face first at estimates of over 50 miles per hour. The blunt force of the impact was devastating to say the least, shattering the bones in her face and in other areas of her body like eggshells. The injuries that Tessa sustained from the impact were not only devastating but life changing as well. The impact left her with a shattered face, losing six teeth, her pelvis bone broken in two places, and with a broken leg.

Though Tessa was left with devastating injuries, she survived the impact. The truth of the matter is that Tessa was not alone when she fell to what easily could have been her death. In fact, God himself was with Tessa every single foot of the 10,000 feet of her fall. Even with all the injuries, God showed favor to Tessa and saw fit for her to survive the impact.

Not only did God show Tessa favor by allowing her to live, He also was faithful and answered her most solemn prayer. Tessa did not remember the sheer horror of impacting the ground. And, as she asked of God, she did not feel the pain of impacting the cold hard blacktop parking lot where she landed.

But Tessa's favor with God does not simply end with her surviving the fall from 10,000 feet without a functional parachute and not feeling the pain from impacting the ground. From this point Tessa's story becomes even more amazing. Not to imply that it is not already amazing enough.

True, Tessa's story thus far is amazing enough, right? She falls 10,000 feet without a functional parachute, hits the ground at 50 miles per hour receiving devastating injuries, yet lives. But there is more to this already unbelievable testament that emerge out of the impending tragedy of this story.

When Tessa's fellow skydivers reached her broken body, she was not just laying there totally unconscious. Tessa was actually trying to get up from her fall and her instructor had to tell her to remain still until rescuers arrived. Tessa was taken by rescuers to a hospital in Fayetteville, Arkansas where she received treatment for her injuries. Most intensive, Tessa's face had to be peeled back, the eggshell pieces of her skull were removed, and fifteen steel plates were inserted where the bone structure of her face once was.

During her treatment for her injuries, doctors discovered that Tessa was pregnant. This of course was news to Tessa as well who would have never gone skydiving in the first place that day if she knew she was pregnant. Not only did she survive the impact, but so did her baby, even after hitting the ground face down at over 50 miles per hour. Medical science tells us that falls from any distance are dangerous for expecting mothers and their unborn fetus. Let alone a fall from over 10,000 feet.

Apparently, even an impact of that magnitude is no match for the human womb when God's favor is in play and His grace and mercy are factored into the equation. The new life inside of Tessa was not aborted as a result of her fall. Tessa gave birth to a healthy 7 pound, 13 ounce baby boy on June 17, 2006.

Through this whole ordeal the most inspiring thing to me is that although Tessa's body was broken, her spirit wasn't. Just a few short weeks after her fall, Tessa demanded to see the video tape of her impacting the ground at over 50 miles per hour. She actually wanted to see it. She said, "I wanted to watch it; and the whole reason I'm comfortable with watching it is because I know how it ends." As if this wasn't enough for you, Tessa actually scheduled her next jump for mid August of 2006.

There is no doubt in my mind that if Tessa would have truly been alone that day she would have died. But she wasn't alone. God was with her and showed her favor as she made her most solemn request made known to Him, even as she faced what she thought was going to be her last few moments on earth. Tessa's parachutes failed her, but God didn't.

If we examine this chapter's guiding scripture closely there is something else that I feel is necessary to at least point out about Tessa through this whole ordeal that is fore-shadowed in the scriptures. It says:

> And they have overcome (conquered) him by means of the blood of the Lamb and by the utterance of their testimony, for they did not love and cling to life even when faced with death [holding their lives cheap till they had to die for their witnessing] (Revelation 12:11, AMP).

Tessa did not cling to life even in the face of death just as those who have overcome by the utterance of their testimony. Even in the face of death she left her fate totally in

God's hands. There is so much we can learn from Tessa's experience.

[Chapter 3]

We Fall Often

"For we all often stumble and fall and offend in many things. . ." (James 3:2, AMP).

Not many of us have the pleasure of being able to say that we have only had one parachute failure and one fall in life. The fact of the matter is that if you have been blessed enough to have been around for any length of time, you have probably had the unfortunate experience of enduring many parachute failures and falling many times. Why is this? Well, it is because the enemy is always on assignment to find ways to sabotage your parachute and set you up for a fall.

We learned that Tessa had jumped and fallen nine times prior to that faithful day when she made that tenth and nearly fatal jump. With her parachute she felt as though she was in control of her fall but it didn't take long for her to realize that no matter how prepared you think you are, you're never truly ready for a fall even if you have fallen many times before. That is because each and every parachute failure and fall that you may experience in life is different with varying degrees of circumstances, impact levels and consequences.

Like Tessa we are too quick to want to put all of our trust into parachutes. We put all of our trust into those life parachutes that we have spent countless hours packing. We trust in our jobs, our education, our relationships, and so forth and we believe that they will open up, pan out, and keep us safe from a life changing fall that can only result in a devastating impact that leaves us hurt and broken. It is not uncommon for us to put all of our heart and all of our trust in life parachutes only to end up heartbroken and wondering what went wrong.

The Holy Spirit through the Word of God tells us exactly what goes wrong and why our parachutes often fail leaving us to fall. It is so simplistic that it is sickening that we could overlook such a minor detail in life. King Solomon, son of David, leaves us with a word of wisdom in Proverbs 3:5-6, which says, "Trust in the LORD with all thine heart; and lean not unto thine own understanding. In all thy ways acknowledge him, and he shall direct thy paths."

I am sure that somebody out there is glad that I finally said it even though it took me a while to get there. We put too much of our hearts and our trust in our parachutes and not enough of our hearts and trust in God! We lean too much on our own understanding of things; we rely too much on our own knowledge, and try to make our own way instead of waiting on God to direct our path. In other words, we jump when we want to jump using the parachutes that we want to use. And, we do it often.

Let's be honest here just for one minute. We put all of our heart and soul into getting a quality education; trusting that it will give us a certain level of social and economic status and it fails us. Now we are left with surmounting student loan debt and no change in social or economic status. Yes, the education parachute can fail us. We put all of our heart into our jobs and careers trusting that someday we will be able to retire with a good pension and not have to work. But one day we go to work and are handed a pink slip to realize we are being laid off after giving fifteen years of our life to our employer. Now there is no pension, no income, no benefits, and we are left starting all over. Yes, the job and career parachutes often fail us. Understand that there is not one life parachute that does not have the potential to fail us.

There are two things that I know for certain. First, remember that the Word of God in Proverbs 3:5-6, tells us to, "Trust in the LORD with all thine heart; and lean not unto thine own understanding. In all thy ways acknowledge him, and he shall direct thy paths." If we put our hearts and our trust in God rather than our life parachutes we will not fall as often because God will not lead us down a path that will require us to use a parachute that will fail us and allow us to fall.

The second thing that I know is that we do fall often and it is almost always a devastating experience that we don't always feel like trying to get up from. But I have learned that the Bible is true when it says in Proverbs 24:16, "For a just man falleth seven times, and riseth up again. . ." Now keep in mind that it does not say that we "only" can fall seven times and rise again. I want you to know that no matter how many times you may fall you can rise again.

You may fall often, but like Tessa you can get back up again. Later we will look at some of the things that Tessa did that not only helped her survive her fall, but gave her the strength to get back up. We are designed to rise again.

[Chapter 4]

We Fall Alone

". . . But woe to him who is alone when he falls and has not another to lift him up!" (Ecclesiastes 4:10, AMP).

Alone! This is a word that stirs many emotions in people for different reasons. For some, to be alone is a scary place to be feared. For others, alone is a place that provides a sanctuary for peace and quiet. Some of us see being alone as a blessing. Others see being alone as a curse. One thing that most of us will agree on is that being alone when we fall and are hurting is not a good place to be. In fact, the book of Ecclesiastes says "woe" to those who are alone when they fall.

If you reflect back to chapter 2 in this book you will remember that Tessa was alone when she jumped, alone when she fell, and alone when she hit the cold hard ground after falling from over 10,000 feet when not one, but two parachutes failed her. As her story begins in chapter 2 we learn that this was her first time making the jump solo. Just to clarify, it was her first time making the jump unassisted and alone. Of all the times to have her parachutes not open, why now?

It is true that there were other skydivers present, observers watching, and when she hit the ground many who rushed to her aid. But, Tessa had to live through the ordeal alone. No one on that day experienced what she experienced. Likewise when life parachutes don't open we are left to fall alone, no one is going through the ordeal the way we are going through it. In fact, even people who have gone through the same type of life parachute failure can only relate, but not truly understand. That is because every fall is different.

I have learned that when we fall in life people tend to shun you. When you are on top of the world everyone is with you, but when you fall and are at the bottom it is hard to find a good friend. What you often find is loneliness. If you are not convinced of this just ask Job. When Job lost everything that he had his wife and friends accused him of being unrighteous, told him that God had left him, and urged him to just go ahead and curse God and die. They told Job to just go ahead and throw in the towel and give up. But Job was innocent and blameless. All along it was old Satan who was sabotaging Job's life parachutes.

If you have never taken the time to read the book of Job in the Bible I would encourage you to do so in the near future. One thing that has always amazed me is that through Job's whole ordeal God still had His hand on Job. The bible says in Job 1:8-12:

And the LORD said unto Satan, Hast thou considered my servant Job, that there is none like him in the earth, a perfect and an upright man, one that feareth God, and scheweth evil? Then Satan answered the LORD, and said, Doth Job fear God for nought? Hast not thou made an hedge about him, and about his house, and about all that he hath on every side? thou hast blessed the work of his hands, and his substance is increased in the land. But put forth thine hand now, and touch all that he hath, and he will curse thee to thy face. And the LORD said unto Satan, Behold, all that he hath is in thy power; only upon himself put not forth thine hand. So Satan went forth from the presence of the LORD.

Satan took everything away from Job but did not touch Job because God had prohibited it. When Job refused to curse God and die Satan made yet another attempt to sabotage the remainder of Job's life parachutes. Again God and

Satan had a conversation concerning Job as recorded in the Bible in the book of Job 2:3-6:

> And the LORD said unto Satan, Hast thou considered my servant Job, that there is none like him in the earth, a perfect and an upright man, one that feareth God, and scheweth evil? and still he holdeth fast his integrity, although thou movedst me against him, to destroy him without cause. And Satan answered the LORD, and said, Skin for skin, yea, all that a man hath will he give for his life. But put forth thine hand now, and touch his bone and his flesh, and he will curse thee to thy face. And the LORD said unto Satan, Behold, he is in thine hand; but save his life.

In both cases God limited what Satan could do to Job. By virtue God had his hand on Job and was with Job through the whole ordeal. When you look at it, Job was never truly alone even when his wife and friends turned their back on him because God Himself was with Job; and God spared Job's life.

I know beyond a shadow of a doubt that when Tessa's parachute failed she was not truly alone. God was with her every inch of all 10,000 feet that she fell. I know this because against all odds she survived and not only did she survive the seed she was carrying, her unborn baby, survived when they both should have been terminated.

When your life parachutes don't open you can be rest assured that even when family and friends are nowhere to be found God is right there with you. Think about all of the things that you have been through, or maybe even that you are going through right now, and yet you are still here. God has not allowed Satan to take your life and is with you even right now.

Always be mindful that just as with Tessa and Job that God is always right there with you. He promises in His word that he will never leave you nor forsake you. In the book of Hebrews God Himself is quoted as making such promise. The book of Hebrews 13:5 says, "Let your conversation be without covetousness; and be content with such things as ye have: for He hath said, I will never leave thee, nor forsake thee." Even when life's parachutes don't open and you find yourself falling through life, be content with your situation because God is with you and He will never leave you or forsake you.

[Chapter 5]

We Fall Fast

". . . And He said to them, I saw Satan falling like a light-ning [flash] from heaven." (Luke 10:18, AMP).

P lease do not be alarmed, I am in no way comparing us to Satan by any stretch of your imagination. Jesus told the disciples that He saw Satan fall from Heaven like a flash of lightning. What Jesus was saying is that Satan's fall from heaven was quick and fast. If you have ever witnessed lightning striking, you will notice that it is quick, powerful, and strikes without notice.

When lightning strikes there is no prior notice and it is almost impossible to get out of the way. Furthermore when lightning strikes something there is always considerable damage left behind. For the record lightning on average travels at an estimated 3,700 miles per second.

There are some things in common with Tessa's fall and a lightning strike. According to reports Tessa hit the ground at an estimated 55 miles per hour. This is no comparison to the speed of a lightning bolt that travels at an estimated

3,700 miles per second, but nevertheless 55 miles per hour is rather fast. Let's be honest, it is faster than any of us can run.

Also, Tessa's fall came without warning just like most lightning strikes happen without warning. She had no idea that day that her jump would result in a life changing fall. Finally, just as when lightning strikes, Tessa's fall resulted in devastating, life-changing consequences.

If you really stop to think about it, when our life parachutes don't open and we find ourselves falling, it happens just like a lightning strike. Often times by the time we realize we are falling we have already fallen. Just as when lightning strikes our falls most of the time happen without any prior notice.

We have no forewarning or even the slightest clue we are about to fall. We are just moving through life as usual, going through everyday tasks, living an everyday normal life, and then it happens. We fall! Just like when lightning strikes we find ourselves damaged. In fact, to use a little bit of urban lingo we can often say we got burnt in the process of falling.

It doesn't take a lot of explanation or cross analysis to see that when we do fall it is very quick. To say that we fall as quickly as lightning flashes may be an exaggeration of the truth, however the similarities between the two events are quite noticeable. There is not a whole lot to say here in this chapter but I just want to make it clear that often when we fall we fall fast and we fall without warning. This in itself is what makes falling often so devastating. The faster you fall, the harder you fall, and the greater the impact on your life. The damage we suffer physically, mentally, and emotionally, is even greater when we don't have the time to prepare and brace ourselves for impact.

If you remember back in chapter 2 I emphasized that the Word of God tells us in the book of Revelation that we can overcome not only by the blood of the Lamb, but also by the utterance of our testimonies (Revelation 12:11). In other words, when we hear of another person's testimony, it gives us the strength to overcome and to conquer the enemy. Well, I can personally testify that when life's parachutes don't open and we find ourselves in a free fall, we fall fast and I don't mind giving you an account of my own personal experience.

At one point in time in my life I had packed several life parachutes that I believed would prevent me from falling in life. I had packed the education parachute, the career parachute, the marriage parachute, and the religion parachute. I truly believed that all these parachutes packed would carry me through life and take me to a place of happily ever after. When you think about it, I had more than a main parachute and a backup parachute packed. I had a main parachute and several reserve parachutes packed at the same time. Like Tessa, I never thought in a million years that all of my parachutes would fail and leave me to fall crashing to the cold ground. When they all failed, they all failed at once and I fell fast.

At one instant I had a stable career, well rounded education, happy marriage, and an ideal church home. Without a moment's notice and in a very short time, as fast as lightning if you will, I was betrayed in my marriage of over twelve years and ended up in divorce, my education endeavours came to a screeching halt, I was being laid off from my job of over fifteen years, my church family was divided and in turmoil, and on top of it all I found myself in bankruptcy. All of this went down in less than an eighteen month period. At that moment, every parachute in life that I was depending on failed at once and I found myself falling on a collision course with a devastating, life changing impact with no way of stopping myself from falling. Then I experienced the impact.

I found myself lying on the cold cruel ground of life. Everything was damaged and I was in pain in every aspect of my life. I was broken in mind, body and spirit. I remember one day just lying on the sofa in my living room; crying and contemplating committing suicide. I wanted all the pain to just end by any means necessary. Satan was really working on me and I was as vulnerable as humanly possible. I had thoughts that told me I would never amount to anything again, that I would never have anything ever again in life and that I would never recover from it all, and the list continued. I was ready and willing to die.

Much like Tessa after her fall I was broken and critically wounded. But, in my darkest hour amidst the shadows of my broken life the Holy Spirit whispered the subtle reminder to my inner man that even though I was broken and wounded I was still alive. I cried out to God late in my midnight hour and my spirit was encouraged in God's Word and from the time tested pages of the Holy Bible I received a command that was confirmation that at all cost I had to get back up. I received revelation just as the Apostle John did on the small island of Patmos and the Spirit of God spoke to me saying, ". . . strengthen the things which remain, that are ready to die: for I have not found thy works perfect before God" (Revelation 3:2). I had been cast down but not destroyed; I was capable of getting back up.

[Chapter 6]

We Are Damaged Not Destroyed

". . . We are struck down to the ground, but never struck out and destroyed" (2 Corinthians 4:9, AMP).

Looking back on Tessa's experience we can all marvel at the mere fact that she survived. Although she was critically injured she was not killed. Another way of looking at it is that although she was damaged in every literal sense she was not destroyed.

I like what the King James Version of the Bible says over in 2 Corinthians 4:8-9 when the Apostle Paul said, "We are troubled on every side, yet not distressed; we are perplexed, but not in despair; Persecuted, but not forsaken; cast down, but not destroyed." One thing that's for sure is that this scripture surely reflects on Tessa's situation at the time of her fall. In the midst of it all she wasn't forsaken. We know that God was with her the entire time. As mentioned before she definitely was not destroyed because she is still alive.

Through my season of great parachute failures it took me a long time to realize that 2 Corinthians 4:8-9 was alive and active in my life. When my life parachutes began to fail one after another I was so preoccupied with all the negativity that I didn't even notice that there was a both positive and promising undertone to my situation. I was actually living the promises of God in 2 Corinthians 4:8-9.

I seemed to be experiencing trouble on every side, but I utterly was not in any severe distress. Yes I had stress, but I was not in distress. I found myself often perplexed, but I was at no time in total despair. I found myself under great persecution at times, but God brought me through it all. In fact, I found myself protected under Psalm 91. I was relentlessly being cast down, enduring fall after fall, but at no point was I every totally destroyed.

Yes, I experienced several of those life changing impacts and was at times critically injured spiritually and emotionally which eventually manifested physically. But I was not destroyed. I was not dead. Like Tessa I was alive, and because I was still alive, I had survived. As a survivor, I had the potential to rise. Can you see 2 Corinthians 4:8-9 at work in your life? Have you seen it at work in your life in the past;

perhaps in the midst of one of your own life parachute failures?

You may have experienced or may be experiencing trouble on every side, but you are not in or most likely have not been in any severe distress. I am sure you find yourself under stress, but you are not totally in distress. You may have found yourself perplexed or may even be perplexed, but total despair is far from you. You may have experienced or may be experiencing great persecution, but God has brought you through before and he will bring you through again. You may have been cast down before or be in the midst of a great fall right now, but at no point have you been or will you find yourself totally destroyed.

Yes, you may have experienced several of those life changing impacts and may be about to experience one right now. You have been or will be critically injured spiritually and emotionally with manifestations of such manifesting physically. But destruction is not for you! Death is not for you! You are alive! You shall live and not die! Because you live, you shall survive! And as long as you survive, you shall arise!

Part II
Survive The Fall And Get Back Up

[Chapter 7]

Cut Loose The Parachutes

". . . for they did not love and cling to life even when faced with death . . ." (Revelation 12:11, AMP).

Too often in life when our life parachutes don't open we still try to hang on to them even though they have proven to fail us and be useless. But, it is human nature to try to hold on to things that are useless to us simply because they are familiar to us. If we think about this for a moment, whatever that life parachute is that we are hanging onto even in the midst of a fall, we are reluctant to let it go because we still believe it is going to open up and save our life. That it is eventually going to stop us from falling. But most of the time this is nothing more than a false hope.

When I reflect back on Tessa's experience, the Holy Spirit leads me to understand that Tessa did not keep hold of her parachutes even when faced with death. In the face of tragedy she made a quick and conscious decision to take her faith and trust out of her parachute and put it into God.

Tessa was unaware that in the process she put her very life into God's hands. Let's look back on Tessa's experience for a moment with some detail.

Suddenly, Tessa was faced with the hard reality that her decent back to earth was not going to be smooth sailing. In an instant, she had to come to the realization that something was going terribly wrong. She heard a snap and started spinning rapidly out of control; gaining acceleration as she began to plummet towards the ground.

When Tessa looked up at her parachute, she discovered that her steering toggle had snapped and her canopy was in danger of totally collapsing which would create an even more life threatening situation. Tessa's trusty parachute, in which she had full faith, had failed putting her very life in danger.

Having been trained for such an emergency, Tessa immediately took action to save her life and cut away her main parachute in preparation to deploy her reserve parachute. Still feeling somewhat confident that she could return back down to earth safely, Tessa then deployed her reserve parachute. As fate would have it, the reserve parachute too failed to properly deploy. Tessa was still falling rapidly out of control towards the ground below. Tessa now very quickly came to the realization that the parachutes that she had once trusted and had full faith in had both failed her.

Tessa was almost in a state of sheer disbelief. First, her main parachute had failed and then her backup chute had failed as well. What were the odds of that happening? Experts agree that the chances of a parachute failing are about one in a million. However, the odds of both parachutes failing are almost nonexistent.

Now falling from initially about 10,000 feet without a functional parachute, Tessa makes one last attempt to break her fall by pumping the brakes on her backup parachute in an effort to get it to fully deploy. When her backup parachute still failed to fully deploy, Tessa began to accept the reality of the grim situation she was in.

Tessa realized that she was in a free fall from 10,000 feet. She realized that she was diving solo, so for all intended purposes she was in fact alone, falling from heights not generally survived. To that end she began to accept the fact that she was most likely going to die in a few short moments.

Having done all that she could at that point to save her-self, Tessa totally let go of her parachute's steering toggles thinking to herself, "I'm going to die. I'm going to hit the ground. I'm going to die." While still falling, Tessa made her petition known to God. She asked God, "Please take away the pain of the impact." She told God, "I am ready to go home, but I just don't want to feel the pain." Having now made her peace with God, accepting that she was going to impact the ground all alone and die, Tessa then laid herself out into a prostrate position, belly-to-earth, closed her eyes, and fell to the earth from 10,000 feet without a functioning parachute.

I know you have heard this all regarding Tessa's experi-ence back in chapter 2, but look at what happens when we take our faith and trust out of our parachutes and put them into God. Plain and simply put, we survive. Tessa was not at all hesitant about cutting away her first parachute and then ultimately letting go of her second parachute even in the face of death. She cut away the only two tangible things known to her that could break her fall and save her life at that moment in time. I know beyond any shadow of a doubt that when Tessa exercised that major act of faith that God honored it and spared her life.

Notice that Tessa did not fall through the air begging and pleading for life. She did not try to hang on to her parachutes, kicking and screaming out like most of us do in the face of tragedy. As they say in church, Tessa simply let go and let God. When your parachutes don't open and you have done all that you can do to break your fall are you willing to just let go and let God? Are you willing to cut loose your parachutes, put your faith and trust in God, and let Him bring you through? Resolve within yourself today that the next time one of life's parachutes fail you that you will cut them loose and put your faith and trust in God and depend on Him for your survival.

[Chapter 8]

Petition God

"Do not fret or have any anxiety about anything, but in every circumstance and in everything, by prayer and petition (definite request), with thanksgiving, continue to make your wants known to God" (Philippians 4:6, AMP).

When we find ourselves in the midst of a great fall as a result of parachute failure our main concern is often on how we are going to survive; how we are going to make it through. We find ourselves full of fear and anxiety and neglect to recognize that even in the midst of our falls we have plenty to be thankful for. Beyond that we often become so busy with our situation that we forget to pray about our situation.

One thing for certain is that when Tessa was in the midst of her fall she did not forget to pray. In fact she talked to God, which is what prayer is, conversation with God, and made her request in what could have been her last moments known to Him. She did not ask God to spare her life.

In fact, she pretty much had accepted the fact that she was going to die that day and go home to be with the Lord. Nevertheless, she made her request known to God and they were granted.

Remember, having done all that she could at that point to save herself, Tessa totally let go of her parachute's steering toggles thinking to herself, "I'm going to die. I'm going to hit the ground. I'm going to die." While still falling, Tessa made her petition known to God. She asked God, "Please take away the pain of the impact." She told God, "I am ready to go home, but I just don't want to feel the pain."

Even though Tessa surrendered to whatever God was going to have happen that day she still made her request known to Him. One thing that I have learned is that God will give us the desires of our heart. In fact Psalm 37:4 says, "Delight thyself also in the Lord: and He shall give thee the desires of thine heart." Tessa asked that she would not feel the pain of the impact. How likely is that?

Tessa landed in a blacktopped parking lot impacting the ground face first at estimates of over 50 miles per hour. The blunt force of the impact was devastating to say the least, shattering the bones in her face and in other areas of her body like eggshells. The injuries that Tessa sustained from the impact were not only devastating but life changing as well. The impact left her with a shattered face, losing six teeth, her pelvis bone broken in two places, and with a broken leg.

Though Tessa was left with devastating injuries, she survived the impact. Even with all the injuries, God showed favor to Tessa and saw fit for her to survive the impact. Not only did God show Tessa favor by allowing her to live, He also was faithful and answered her most solemn petition. Tessa did not remember the sheer horror of impacting the ground. And, as she asked of God, she did not feel the pain of impacting the cold hard blacktop parking lot where she landed.

What we can learn from Tessa's actions is that when old Satan sabotages our parachutes we can make our petitions known to God as to how we would like for things to turn out. We can ask God to take away the pain, to lessen the damage, to heal us, to restore things in our lives, or whatever else is in our hearts. One thing that we must continue to remember is that it is God's desire for us to survive our falls, recover, get up, have the victory and be able to give Him all of the glory, honor, and praise.

I will leave you with one last thought in this chapter. The Bible says in John 16:24, ". . . ask, and you shall receive. . ." God gives us permission to ask of Him what we want. Even in the midst of our falls and especially in our gravest hours God hears our prayers and will not forsake us. Make up in your mind today that when life's parachutes fail you, you can make your petitions known to Him and have trust and faith that He will deliver you from the impact of your fall according to how you have requested.

[Chapter 9]

Prepare For Impact

"And going a little farther, He threw Himself upon the ground on His face and prayed saying, My Father, if it is possible, let this cup pass away from Me; nevertheless, not what I will [not what I desire], but as You will and desire."
(Matthew 26:39, AMP).

It seems impossible at times to prepare for what life is going to throw at you. No matter how much training Tessa had undergone prior to the day of her accident, she could have never in a million years been totally prepared for what she had to endure. What amazes me to this day is that in the book of Matthew we find an account of Jesus Himself preparing for what He was about to endure.

Once Tessa came to grips with the hard reality that she was going to fall to the ground there were some things that she did to make preparation for what was about to happen. In Chapter 7 we learned that Tessa enacted her faith, and cut loose her parachutes. In Chapter 8 we learned that

Tessa made her petition known to God. But there is one more thing that Tessa did that the Holy Spirit revealed to me that we need to do when our life parachutes don't open and we find ourselves falling to an impending death.

According to my account of Tessa's story in Chapter 2, when she had made her peace with God, accepting that she was going to impact the ground all alone and die, Tessa then laid herself out into a prostrate position, belly-to-earth, closed her eyes, and fell to the earth from 10,000 feet without a functioning parachute. Much like Jesus in Matthew 26:39, Tessa laid herself into a prostrate position totally submitting herself to God's will; totally putting herself in God's hands.

When was the last time in the midst of a devastating fall that you have laid yourself prostrate before God? If Jesus and Tessa in their darkest hours humbled themselves to lay prostrate before God and totally submitted to whatever outcome that God had in store for them, why can we not do the same? In the midst of a fall lay yourself prostrate, belly-to-earth, and let God set you in the position he desires for you to be in. You will find yourself in a much better position than the one your parachute would put you in.

[Chapter 10]

Fall Into God's Hands

"And David said to Gad, I am in great distress. Let us fall into the hands of the Lord . . ." (II Samuel 24:14, AMP).

Something about falling leaves us in a certain state of distress. This was a feeling that King David knew all too well. I know when my parachutes in life failed me the whole ordeal left me in a moderate state of distress. Likewise when Tessa's parachutes failed her I am sure for a short moment she was feeling rather distressed.

When you fall in the natural sense, where you land determines how severe your injuries will be. Falling on a concrete slab does much more damage than falling in the grass. Falling in the grass can be much more harmful than falling in a pool of water. One thing that David believed is that there was no better place to fall than into the hands of God. And I must say that I agree with King David 100%.

David had an understanding that there was a certain degree of safety involved with falling into the hands of God.

David wrote in Psalms 37:23-24, "Though he fall, he shall not be utterly cast down: for the Lord upholdeth him with His hands." When you fall into God's hands God upholds you and even in the midst of your fall you will not be cast down.

Tessa landed in a blacktopped parking lot impacting the ground face first at estimates of over 50 miles per hour. The blunt force of the impact was devastating to say the least, shattering the bones in her face and in other areas of her body like eggshells. The injuries that Tessa sustained from the impact were not only devastating but life changing as well. The impact left her with a shattered face, losing six teeth, her pelvis bone broken in two places, and with a broken leg.

Though Tessa was left with devastating injuries, she survived the impact. The truth of the matter is that Tessa was not alone when she fell to what easily could have been her death. In fact, God himself was with Tessa every single foot of the 10,000 feet of her fall and even though she made impact with the ground, she fell into the hands of the Lord. I know this because even with all the injuries, God showed favor to Tessa and saw fit for her to survive the impact. She was not utterly cast down. So how did Tessa manage to fall into the hands of the Lord?

It is the same principle that we have heard before. Remember the petition that Tessa made to God. Having done all that she could at that point to save herself, Tessa totally let go of her parachute's steering toggles thinking to herself, "I'm going to die. I'm going to hit the ground. I'm going to die." While still falling, Tessa made her petition known to God. She asked God, "Please take away the pain of the impact." She told God, "I am ready to go home, but I just don't want to feel the pain."

Having now made her peace with God, accepting that she was going to impact the ground all alone and die, Tessa then laid herself out into a prostrate position, belly-to-earth, closed her eyes, and fell to the earth from 10,000 feet without a functioning parachute. It was her petition to God and her subsequent actions that put her into a position to fall into God's hands and survive the impact with the hard ground below.

One thing that I know about most of us is that when life's parachutes don't open and we find ourselves falling we are willing to land almost anywhere as long as we get our feet back on the ground. However, we are very reluctant to be willing to just simply fall into the hands of the Lord. Why is that do you think? Well, the bible tells us in the book of Hebrews 10:31 that, "It is a fearful thing to fall into the hands of the living God." What are we afraid of? Why are we so reluctant to allow ourselves to fall into the hands of the Lord?

The Holy Spirit has shown me that the reason why most of us do not want to end up in the hands of God is because in spite of what we say about wanting to be in God's will and in the position He would have us be in, we are not at all comfortable with it. But the reality is that if we must fall, the best place for us to land is in the hands of God. You would think after going through whatever it is that you have had to endure at Satan's hands that you would be more than happy to wake up in God's hands. As part of your petition to God, try saying, "God, if I must fall and there is no way that this fall can be prevented, let me to fall into your hands."

[Chapter 11]

Remember From Where You Fall

"Remember then from what heights you have fallen.
Repent (change the inner man to meet God's will) . . ."
(Revelation 2:5, AMP).

Remember from where you fall. When life's parachutes fail to open and we fall to the ground with life changing impact, the last thing we want to do is remember any of the details. We have already endured a great deal of emotional, spiritual, and even physical pain and now we are seeking to summon up mental pain and suffering as well. We can only imagine what Tessa went through but this young woman's story continues to amaze me.

Through Tessa's whole ordeal the most inspiring thing to me is that although Tessa's body was broken, her spirit wasn't. Just a few short weeks after her fall, Tessa demanded to see the video tape of her impacting the ground at over 50 miles per hour. She actually wanted to see it. She said, "I wanted to watch it; and the whole reason I'm comfortable with watching it is because I know how it ends." As if this wasn't enough for you, Tessa actually scheduled her next jump for mid August of 2006.

Tessa actually wanted to see herself falling because she wanted to remember from where she fell from. This actually helped Tessa finish her recovery process. The Bible in Revelation 2:5 says, "Remember therefore from whence thou art fallen, and repent, and do the first works. . ." The key word here is to repent, which means to turn away from. Why is this so important? It is important because we all need to learn to turn away from those parachutes that have caused us to fall in the first place. We need to learn to stop putting our faith and trust in parachutes and put our faith and trust in God.

I know how hard this can be. Who wants to sit back and remember all the things in life that have let us down? To remember all the parachutes that have been sabotaged by Satan in our lives that resulted in us falling to the ground with life changing impact. Most of us have fallen before and to some degree we know how certain falls are going to turn out. Think about what Tessa said about wanting to watch her fall. She said, "I wanted to watch it; and the whole reason I'm comfortable with watching it is because I know how it ends."

Every fall that you have had in life is no surprise to you. You know how it ends. You know what the results are but yet it is so tempting to just ponder within yourself and say, "I don't want to think about it or talk about it; I just don't want to relive it." But here is a little word of wisdom for you to really let get down in your spirit.

If you allow yourself to remember from where you have fallen and reflect on what parachutes in your life Satan can so easily sabotage; you are less likely to put your faith and trust in those types of parachutes in the future. I am not saying you should never trust again or have faith in anything but God. I am just saying that you should have more faith and trust in God than anything else.

I really like what the Amplified Bible says in Revelation 2:5 because of the clarification it makes when it says for us to, "Remember then from what heights you have fallen. Repent (change the inner man to meet God's will). . ." Change the inner man to meet God's will! The "inner man" is your soul and spirit. Change your inner man to meet God's will. Now that is a powerful statement.

I am inclined to believe that when we are in God's will for our life, Satan cannot sabotage our parachutes. I know that from the beginning of this book we have given Satan all or at least most of the credit for our parachutes not doing what they are suppose to do but if we are going to be real with ourselves then we must acknowledge that in some cases it has been our own actions that have allowed Satan to sabotage our parachutes. Enough said about that. That is another whole book for a different time. Dare to remember from where you have fallen. Resolve to change your inner man to meet God's will for your life.

[Chapter 12]

Now Get Back Up

"For a righteous man falls seven times and rises again . . ."
(Proverbs 24:16, AMP).

From the very beginning I have expressed that the hardest part about falling in life is getting back up. Over the years I have encountered many people who have fallen and have yet to get back up. To make matters worse, they have not even begun the process of getting back up. I myself have even been one of those people.

Our initial reaction to a fall of great magnitude is that we are just going to stay down. We are finished, not getting up; we are complacent to just stay where we are. No matter, we will just find a bigger and better parachute. That's what we say right?

The hardest part about falling in any given situation is getting back up. That is because when we fall, we often get hurt in the process and end up either wounded or injured. There is no doubt that falling is often a traumatic experience for most of us. However, one thing that is for certain is that a fall is a prerequisite for an opportunity to get back up. We can never have an opportunity to get back up if we first don't fall. Let's take a look at it in retrospect of our parachute failures.

All too often our parachutes fail to deploy and we find ourselves free falling out of control towards the cold hard ground below. The things that we trust most; our education, careers, friendships, marriages, businesses, and even our religious affiliations fail to fully open up. Our parachutes fail to carry us to that safe place; that place of happily ever after where we expect to land. As a result, we inevitably hit the ground of reality with blunt force and life changing impact.

Upon impact, we find ourselves broken, wounded, and full of devastation. We find ourselves in immense pain. We are critically injured emotionally, spiritually, psychologically, and sometimes even physically. The blunt force of the impact leaves us lifeless in so many ways and in a lame position.

With the life knocked out of us, we have little to no desire to be moved, let alone get up. We find ourselves in critical condition, on spiritual life support, laid out in the intensive care unit of disappointment. As we begin to recover we often have little to no desire to leap out on faith towards the adventurous things in life ever again. We simply don't have much faith in those all alluring life parachutes anymore that we once trusted. Simply stated, we are not thinking about getting back up.

The post traumatic effect is almost unbearable because many of us have been taught that as children of God life will be so much better than where we are now. That everything will always be just fine because we are the righteousness of God. We forget that the word of God warns us that, "Many are the afflictions of the righteous . . ." (Psalm 34:19).

While contemplating if we really want to get back up and risk another fall, Satan gets real busy in hindering our recovery. Satan will tell us that we can't do it, that we cant get back up. We begin to believe that we will never be whole again, that we will never be able to get back on our feet, that we will never find happiness, that we will never amount to anything and the list goes on and on. Keep in mind that there is a 100% chance that Satan has already played a part in our fall to begin with one way or another.

The Gospel according to John tells us that, "The thief cometh not, but for to steal, and to kill, and to destroy..." (John 10:10). In the shadows of our traumatic experiences Satan would have us to remain in a broken, wounded, and in a depressed and devastated state of existence. Satan's intention is to magnify our pain, increase our suffering, and steal from us any desire to rise above life's tragedies and walk in the fullness and abundance of God's purpose for our lives.

When our parachutes don't open, it is God's desire for us to survive the impact, arise from the devastation, heal, and prepare for our next leap of faith into life's great adventures. It is God's will that we be made whole again, get back up, and experience all the peace, joy, and happiness that life has to offer. In the same passage of scripture, the Gospel according to John gives us assurance from Jesus Christ who says, "... I came that they might have life, and that they might have it more abundantly." (John 10:10).

We can have all of what God promises but we have got to get back up, no matter how many times we fall. Getting back up is much more significant and extends much deeper than just you and I. Let me explain to you why getting back up is so significant.

It doesn't take divine discernment or any advanced theological knowledge to recognize that we are living in the last days and that time is winding up. The Bible prophesies that in the last days there will be a great outpouring of the Holy Spirit and almost everyone is waiting for it in great anticipation. So where is this outpouring of the Holy Spirit that the church is waiting for; what's the hold up?

After all it is prophesied in the Bible and promises to change church as we have come to know it. Acts 2:17-18 tells us that:

> And it shall come to pass in the last days, saith God, I will pour out of my Spirit upon all flesh: and your sons and your daughters shall prophesy, and your young men shall see visions, and your old men shall dream dreams; And on my servants and on my handmaidens I will pour out in those days of my Spirit; and they shall prophesy.

We are crying out for this great outpouring and in so many ways asking God to let it "rain" upon us. We want a fresh anointing; a word from heaven, deeper discernment, showers of blessings, great revivals and the list goes on and on. The Holy Spirit has given me a Word that not only answers why, but provides a solution. This Word from God is a revelation that even though we say we want this great outpouring of the Holy Spirit; the truth is that we are not ready for it and God has shown me why!

In Genesis 2:5 Moses records historical insight to this revelation saying:

> And every plant of the field before it was in the earth, and every herb of the field before it grew: for the LORD God had not caused it to rain upon the earth, and there was not a man to till the ground.

God had not caused it to "rain" upon the earth because there was no man in existence to till the ground. To put it plain and simple, man was not in the position that God needed for him to be in for there to be rain upon the earth. Likewise, we are not in the position today that God needs for us to be in for Him to allow a great downpour. As a whole we are in what I must call a down, fallen, or lame position.

God needs for us to focus on getting back up and into the position that He needs for us to be in. When God does pour out His Spirit He needs for us to be in an upright position ready to help usher in the harvest of souls that the rain will water, nourish, and help introduce them to a new life in Christ Jesus.

The Holy Spirit brought to my remembrance the story about a certain man over in the book of Acts. We can find his story in Acts 3:2-7 which says:

> And a certain man lame from his mother's womb was carried, whom they laid daily at the gate of the temple which is called Beautiful, to ask alms of them that entered into the temple; who seeing Peter and John about to go into the temple asked an alms. And Peter, fastening his eyes upon him with John, said, Look on us. And he gave heed unto them, expecting to receive something of them. Then Peter said, Silver and gold have I none; but such as I have give I thee: In the name of Jesus Christ of Nazareth rise up and walk. And he took him by the right hand, and lifted him up: and immediately his feet and ankle bones received strength.

There was nothing wrong with this man according to the Bible with the exception that he had weak feet and ankle bones that prohibited him from getting up and being a productive member of society. The enemy sabotaged a particular area of his life from birth and for many years he would lay at the gates daily in a lame position begging to receive something; anything that he could get.

But then on that faithful afternoon this man who was lame at the gate encountered Peter and John who gave him more than he anticipated that day. They gave him a touch from God in the name of Jesus Christ of Nazareth that set him in an upright position to go leaping and praising God. On that day his life was changed forever. On that day, in the name of Jesus, he got up!

The main difference between the man at the gate and us is that he was born into this world in a lame position and we at some point fall into a lame position. Our lame position is the result of a fall that we take in life and fail to get back up from. We too can get back up and into the position that God wants us to be in. Just as the man at the gate got up in the name of Jesus we too should be getting up in the name of Jesus. Believe it or not, the man who was lame at the gate ended up in the position God needed for him to be in.

He moved into a position where he was able to go leaping and praising God.

By natural design and genetic composition we are made to get back up when we fall. The problem is that all too often we fall, but don't get back up. If we don't get back up we are not in the position that God needs for us to be in. Often times when we fall, in our minds we believe that we are getting back up or have already gotten back up. But In reality, we just learn to adapt to our new found down position. Today, let's determine in our minds to get back up.

Let's start by one last time reflecting back on Tessa's experience. Remember, Tessa's story thus far is amazing enough, right? She falls 10,000 feet without a functional parachute, hits the ground at 50 miles per hour receiving devastating injuries, yet lives. But here is the thing that I want to pull out of Tessa's story at this point in time. When Tessa's fellow skydivers reached her broken body, she was not just laying there totally unconscious. Tessa was actually trying to get up from her fall; her instructor had to tell her to remain still until rescuers arrived.

If Tessa was actually trying to get up from a fall of the magnitude that she endured then what is wrong with us that we are so reluctant and so slow to try and get back up? Please don't answer that question; I don't want to open up a can of worms at this point in time. You have been given permission by God to get back up. Remember that Proverbs 24:16 says, "For a just man falleth seven times, and riseth up again. . ."

So far in part two of this book we have learned that to get up from our falls when life's parachutes don't open we first have to survive the fall. We know that sometimes we have to cut loose the parachutes. We know that we have to petition God. We have to prepare ourselves for impact. We must be willing to fall into God's hands. And finally, we need to remember from where we fell. So, how do we ever get back up now that we have survived the fall?

The Holy Spirit laid before me a simplistic, yet empowering, revelation regarding getting back up after we experience one of life's parachute failures. What amazes me is that it is a process that consists of seven steps and to make things simple I am going to present them to you as God intends for me to, as steps.

Step one. In order to get back up we need to be strong and courageous and stand against the enemy. Satan cannot do anything to you that you don't allow him to do. Stand strong on Deuteronomy 31:6 which says, "Be strong and of a good courage, fear not, nor be afraid of them: for the Lord thy God, he it is that doth go with thee; he will not fail thee, nor forsake thee." You have no reason to fear getting back up because God is with you and he will not forsake you. You are not alone!

Step two. We need to realize that the Holy Spirit gives us the power to get back up and that when we decide to get back up Satan cannot stop us. 1 John 4:4 says, "Ye are of God, little children, and have overcome them: because greater is he that is in you, than he that is in the world." The Holy Spirit that dwells within you is greater than Satan, the ruler of this world, and as a result you can take authority over Satan and can overcome whatever Satan has done to you. You are in control!

Step three. We need to stop thinking like the world who says we cannot get back up and start thinking that we can. Understand that Proverbs 23:7 says, "For as he thinketh in his heart, so is he. . ." so if you think in your heart that you can't get back up then you are right. You can't. Therefore you must renew your way of thinking. The Apostle Paul tells us in Romans 12:2, "And be not conformed to this world: but be ye transformed by the renewing of your mind, that ye may prove what is that good, and acceptable, and perfect, will of God." The world would have you believe that you can't get back up, but by renewing your mind you can not only get back up but also prove that which is good and get into the perfect will of God.

Step four. Once we begin to think the right way it is time we start speaking our getting up into existence. Yes, we have the power to do that. Proverbs 18:21 says, "Death and life are in the power of the tongue." We speak where we are into existence by what we say. If we speak we are getting back up, then we are. Even if we are in a fallen state we can speak we are up by faith. Again the Apostle Paul gives us some insight in Romans 4:17 which says, ". . . and calleth those things which be not as though they were." If you are in a lame and fallen position, just proclaim that you are in an upright position.

Step five. We need to recognize that just as Tessa survived the fall and was alive, so are we. If you go back to chapter two and read the latter half of her story you will discover that in spite of her injuries there was lots that remained including her unborn child. Whatever you have left after your fall, take it, strengthen it, rebuild and go forth.

Revelation 3:2 says, "Be watchful, and strengthen the things which remain, that are ready to die: for I have not found thy works perfect before God." Although you may feel you are about to die strengthen yourself, that which remains in you, because God still has work for you to do. Strengthen up and straighten up!

Step six. Stop! Stop! Stop! Stop making excuses why you can't get back up and just do it. It never ceases to amaze me that it is human nature to make excuses rather than take action. If you want to get back up you have got to take some action. Romans 1:20 in the Amplified Bible says, "For ever since the creation of the world His invisible *nature and attributes*, that is, His eternal power and divinity, have been made intelligible *and* clearly discernible in *and* through the things that have been made (His handiworks). So [men] are without excuse [altogether without any defense or justification]." You are now without excuse. So stop making excuses as to why you can't get back up and just do it!

Step seven, the final step. The last thing we have to do is claim the victory over Satan and declare that we have gotten back up. Do you realize that before you even start the battle to get back up, God has already given you the promise that you will rise back up. You are the one that will ultimately rejoice in victory, not Satan. You are the one who will stand victorious in the light of God.

I can personally testify to this because if you recall I mentioned earlier that I went through a period in life when every parachute that I packed in life; my primary parachute and backup parachutes alike were sabotaged by Satan and I found myself in a repetitive, fast free fall. Not only did I hit the ground with devastating life changing impact, I hit it over and over again with each impact more devastating than before, all within an eighteen month period.

Little did I know then that God was with me in every fall and that the Holy Spirit was directing me in my recovery. The same steps that Tessa took are the same steps that I took to get back up and are the same steps that you can take also.

Any time, any place, whenever you get ready; you can speak to Satan directly and tell him in the words of the prophet Micah, "Rejoice not against me, O mine enemy: when I fall, I shall arise; when I sit in darkness, the LORD shall be a light unto me." (Micah 7:8). You can take authority over your life and declare that you are getting back up. Now that you have read this book you have no excuse not to get back up from your falls in life. Now, get back up!

[Conclusion]

God Meant It For Good

Conclusion, already? When I look at what has already been said so far there is not too much more that I can say. In fact, the Holy Spirit really wants me to only say one more thing here. This is kind of tough for me because I have always been trained to write these all conclusive, heroic type of conclusions that sum things all up, but not this time.

One question that I know plagues the mind of many is why would God allow Satan to sabotage our life parachutes causing us to fall with such painful, devastating, life changing impact. Then He reminds me of the story of Joseph whose story is recorded in the book of Genesis. Joseph was betrayed by his brothers, sold into slavery, falsely accused in Egypt and thrown in prison, but eventually arose victorious.

You see, Satan sabotaged Joseph's life in a major way. But glory be to God everything that Joseph went through was ultimately a part of God's divine plan. Likewise, the fall that Tessa took is really a part of God's grand plan. After all, her experience provided a testimony that became a foca point for this book. The falls that I had to undergo in life had a purpose as well. They gave me the insight and understanding that qualified me to write this book. As a great pastor once told me, my falls and experiences validated my anointing.

I don't know what life parachutes have failed you in life. I don't know exactly what falls you have endured in life as a result of your failed parachutes. But the one last thing that the Holy Spirit wants me to relay to you is that no matter what your situation may be God is still in control. God wants me to give you this one more Word that you can speak to Satan:

"As for you, you thought evil against me, but God meant it for good, to bring about that many people should be kept alive, as they are this day."

(Genesis 50:20, AMP).

[Appendix]

Scripture Listing

Preface

Matthew 24:3-14

Acts 2:17-18

Genesis 2:5

Prologue

Acts 3:2-7

Introduction

Psalm 34:19

John 10:10

Proverbs 24:16

Micah 7:8

Chapter 1

Proverbs 4:7, AMP

Chapter 2

Revelation 12:11, AMP

Revelation 12:11

Chapter 3

James 3:2, AMP

Proverbs 3:5-6

Proverbs 24:16

Chapter 4

Ecclesiastes 4:10, AMP

Job 1:8-12

Job 2:3-6

Hebrews 13:5

Chapter 5

Luke 10:10, AMP

Revelation 12:11

Revelation 3:2

Chapter 6

2 Corinthians 4:9, AMP

2 Corinthians 4:8-9

Psalm 91

Chapter 7

Revelation 12:11, AMP

Chapter 8

Philippians 4:6, AMP

Psalm 37:4

John 16:24

Chapter 9

Matthew 26:39, AMP

Chapter 10

II Samuel 24:14, AMP

Psalm 37:23-24

Hebrews 10:31

Chapter 11

Revelation 2:5, AMP

Revelation 2:5

Chapter 12

Proverbs 24:16, AMP

Psalm 34:19

John 10:10

Acts 2:17-18

Genesis 2:5

Acts 3:2-7

Proverbs 24:16

Deuteronomy 31:6

1 John 4:4

Proverbs 23:7

Romans 12:2

Proverbs 18:21

Romans 4:17

Revelation 3:2

Romans 1:30, AMP

Micah 7:8

Conclusion

Genesis 50:20, AMP

D r. Myron Raney is available for speaking engagements including sermons, seminars, lectures, workshops and conferences. He is also readily available for fundraisers, book signings, and other social events. For more information or to book Dr. Raney for your event contact:

Opulent Vision Management
Ms. Lisa Tye, Publicist
(404) 337-4054
www.opulentvisionmgt.com